The Mystery of Weakness

By Bob Mumford

LIFECHANGERS ®

P.O. Box 3709 ❖ Cookeville, TN 38502
931.520.3730 ❖ lc@lifechangers.org

Bob Sutton's editing was instrumental in helping me put together the pieces of this Plumbline. Bob nurtures the body of Christ as a pastor and educator. He served many years as an editor of *New Wine* magazine. I would like to express my gratitude for his friendship and his assistance with this Plumbline.

Unless otherwise noted, all Scripture quotations are taken from *The New American Standard Bible*, The Lockman Foundation, 1960, 1962, 1963, 1968, 1972, 1973, 1975, 1977. All rights reserved.

PLUMBLINE

Published by:

LIFECHANGERS ®
LIBRARY SERIES

P.O. Box 3709 | Cookeville, TN 38502
(800) 521-5676 | www.lifechangers.org

Introduction

The concepts of this *Plumbline* are difficult and challenging to adequately express. They have risen from a deep and exceedingly personal, ongoing journey that Father has entrusted to me in recent years. Part of my journey is rooted in pondering Jesus' statement that we must become like children if we are to enter the Kingdom of God.

The ways of the Kingdom of God have been a major focus of my ministry for 70 years. Jesus' emphasis on the Kingdom and childlikeness has always been somewhere in my thinking. However, it has only been recently that the Lord has been opening to me the breadth of these implications for our spiritual reality. Amazingly, I have gained a new understanding of the spiritual significance of *human weakness.*

Please believe me, "weakness" is not a theme I would have chosen or wished to experience! I would much rather be giving you "The Seven Keys to Purpose, Peace, and Prosperity." Check it out on Amazon or YouTube and you will find an abundant supply.

As the Lord has been faithful to open this enigmatic theme of weakness to me, I am discovering mysteries and paradoxes by which His Kingdom comes. Some of you have endured, or are presently enduring, inexplicable seasons of suffering, loss, and pain. It is my fervent prayer and hope that through what I will be writing you will begin to have a new perspective on your circumstances. I cannot promise miraculous deliverance from your difficulties, but I do know by my own experience that you will grow in wisdom and intimacy. May you see the Father's hand afresh in your life.

I would like to introduce five concepts that are increasingly urgent and demanding. If you are able to see and embrace these, they will help give you clarity and confidence to embrace the inexorable tide rising around us.

First. Jesus' call that we become childlike is more foundational to entering the Kingdom of God than we have been able to comprehend. We will expand this as we go, but being childlike is a spiritual stance. It is essential yet almost impossible to attain by our own effort.

Second. There is a Spiritual validity for experiencing weakness. "Weak" or "weakness" is mentioned thirty-three times in the New Testament. It is a subtle thread woven through the entirety of Scripture. Weakness is often experienced or portrayed in narrative rather than in direct declaration. For this reason, it is often overlooked as an important part of the bigger picture.

Third. Weakness in different forms is often necessary and profitable in the Father's unchanging, predestined purpose to conform us to the image of His Son. This truth is so familiar to us, we often do not fully grasp how critical transformation is to God's focus for all of history. Redemption urges the nations to come under the Kingdom of Christ. Transformation encompasses the redemption of Creation, the earthly establishment of the New Jerusalem, and the final defeat of Darkness. A body of multi-member image-bearing, mature sons and daughters is indispensable.

Fourth. Our ultimate warfare is being fought in the spiritual universe. Dark, fallen entities wage an age-long battle against God and His people. We see the blatant manifestations of these evils in the news media. We are less familiar with the underlying "culture" that permeates the fallen cosmos. It has become common place and is accepted as normal.

Fifth. Weakness can be a powerful, counterintuitive posture for neutralizing the influences of darkness. Understanding and embracing our weakness in the proper context is of utmost importance for ourselves and the body of Christ.

May the Holy Spirit give us revelation and grace as we plunge ahead!

Bring Me the Children

> Truly I say to you, unless you are converted
> and become like children, you will not enter
> the kingdom of heaven.[1]

For many years I have pondered Jesus'
statement to His disciples that unless they become
childlike, they could not enter, let alone function in,
the Kingdom of God. We tend to brush past Jesus'
instruction without catching the gravity of what the
Father is asking of us. Jesus said we need to "be
converted." The Greek is "turned" implying that we
are going the wrong direction. Without trying to be
too technical, "converted" is grammatically in the
passive voice. It is something that may need to be
done to us or for us, rather than by us.

Jesus was somewhat adamant about this with His
disciples. In Mark's gospel He tells them, "Permit
the children to come to Me; do not hinder them; for
the kingdom of God belongs to such as these. Truly
I say to you, whoever does not receive the kingdom
of God like a child will not enter it at all."[2]

It is important to note that entering the Kingdom
of God is not automatic. As shocking as it may be,
we do not automatically enter the Kingdom of God
through the new birth. Jesus makes four statements
in the gospels qualifying the entrance into the

---

1 Matthew 18:3
2 Mark 10:14-15

Kingdom, which I will list without elaborating:

1. Become childlike (Matthew 18:3; Mark 10:15)
2. Have righteousness which exceeds that of the Scribes and Pharisees (Matthew 5:20)
3. Do the will of His Father (Matthew 7:21)
4. Be born of water and the Spirit (John 3:5)

Peter wrote to New Testament believers that "all diligence" should be applied to maturing in eight progressive spiritual qualities. "For in this way," he concluded, "the entrance into the eternal kingdom of our Lord and Savior Jesus Christ will be abundantly supplied to you."[3] These believers had experienced the new birth but were still in the process of maturing into the fullness of the Kingdom of God.

Paul admonished the disciples of the Lord, "Through many tribulations we must enter the Kingdom of God."[4] Jesus told Nicodemus that the new birth enables us to "see" the Kingdom but entering is a process of maturing in obedience.

If we are willing to take Jesus seriously about becoming childlike, we will find He is offering us insight about how God chooses to redemptively approach darkened humanity through the incarnation of the Christ. Childlikeness is an essential stance for allowing the Spirit to begin our transformation as

---

3 From 2 Peter 1:5-11 [Emphasis added]
4 Acts 14:22

mature sons and daughters after the image of the Pattern Son.

Innocence

Why would the Father give revelation to "babes" rather than to the wise and intelligent? "Babes" do not ask for proof texts and challenge the wisdom of the Creator of the Universe. I am reminded of Moses' encounter at the burning bush when the Lord told Moses, "I will send you to Pharoah." Moses challenged the Lord three times, until finally "the anger of the Lord burned against Moses."[5] It is a "pleasure" for the Father to reveal His truth to innocent "babes." He doesn't get a barrage of back talk!

Jesus told His followers that their return to *spiritual innocence* was an indispensable condition in His emerging Kingdom. Innocence, as it being used here, is not primarily a moral state meaning without guilt. Rather, it is used twice in the New Testament as harmless or unsuspecting. If you tell your young children you are going to the amusement park, they will probably not pelt you with questions like: "Do you have enough money?"; "Is there gas in the car?"; or "Will the rides be safe?" No, they will be excited simply because their parents declared it. They believe their parents can handle everything necessary for the outing.

---

5 Exodus 4:14

Trust

In a healthy family, children develop an unwavering trust in their parents. A basic reason is that their needs are met at the initiative of their parents. They need not beg or plead. Jesus reiterated this when He said, "Your Father knows what you need before you ask Him[6] . . . your heavenly Father knows you need all these things."[7]

Desire to Please

Children have a desire to please their parents and experience their approbation. It is part of their developing identity. Sometimes it has unintended consequences. My son once cleaned the ice off my car with a metal scraper, taking some of the paint with it. He was proud of his accomplishment. And despite my sinking heart, I could not get angry with him because I knew his desire was to please me. If our hearts are fixed on pleasing the Lord, He will give grace in our immaturity and ignorance.

Healthy Fear

I want to emphasize the word "healthy." There is a damaging fear that parents may instill by wrathful, inconsistent, and shaming interactions with their children. Tragically, this fear often ends up being projected onto God. Healthy fear allows parents to teach boundaries, respect, and obedience.

The healthy fear of the Lord is one of the most

6 Matthew 6:8
7 Matthew 6:25

common themes of the Scriptures. It promises an astonishing array of benefits. Isaiah prophesied that six manifestations of the Spirit of the Lord would rest on the Messiah. The sixth was the spirit of the fear of the Lord. "And" Isaiah wrote, "He will delight in the fear of the Lord."[8]

Mary, the mother of Jesus, demonstrated a childlike posture toward the angel Gabriel when he declared his astounding message. Her response: "I am the bondservant of the Lord, let it be as you have spoken." Mary must have had a lot of questions at this point, but she kept them to herself. She maintained her innocence, expressed in her humility.

Mary's childlikeness provided for Christ's birth in obscurity and safety. In quiet simplicity, Mary repeatedly operated in freedom from the influence of pride. She was not motivated by an illegal recognition. She stewarded well the motherhood of the Messiah of Israel.

In contrast, the religious and political principalities and powers that surrounded her were infected with the desire for grandeur and illegal recognition. Tragically, they were blinded to the Messiah God sent. They desired one who would fulfill their ambition for recognition in His Kingdom. They longed for the glorious, warrior son of David.

Without education or sophistication, Mary had a better grasp of the Kingdom of God than

8 Isaiah 11:3

the Pharisees, priests, and scholars of first century Judaism. She understood the implications of her calling and walked in humility without the need for greater explanation. For this reason, in her heavenly Father's eyes, she was "highly favored."

Mary declared the mystery of the Kingdom to her cousin, Elizabeth:

> He has had regard for the humble state of His bondslave. He has scattered those who were proud in the thoughts of their heart. He has brought down rulers from their thrones and has exalted those who were humble.[9]

She understood how to function in the Kingdom and how to walk humbly before God. Mary serves as a powerful model for us today.

Why Weakness?

Go to your favorite bookstore or local library and ask for a book on *How to Become Weak*. I promise you will be met with a blank stare, perhaps a laugh. Amazon or Google? Nothing—I checked! We fear weakness. Weakness makes us feel vulnerable. Weakness is disdained. We try to cover it up, deny it, or compensate for it. We strive to become stronger in order to escape it.

In human culture, strength has always been a principal virtue. The strong survive, conquer, lead, and become our heroes. How many times have

---

9 Luke 1:48-52

we been admonished to "be strong," "get over it," "never quit," "stiffen our upper lips," or "put some steel in our backbones?" *Why then would human weaknesses be something our Heavenly Father desires to receive?* In certain situations, we are to welcome human weakness as a necessity. Embracing weakness can become a mysterious spiritual launching pad for the freedom required to enter and mature in the Kingdom of God.

Martin Luther, the father of the Protestant Reformation, knew weakness. In his demanding journey, personal crises, and the unexpected happenings, he identified human weakness (physical, emotional, or circumstantial) as a hidden aspect of the Kingdom. One of my seminary professors stated that Luther identified the circumstances leading to recognition of our weakness as *"God's alien gift"*.

Acknowledging weakness increases dependence on the grace and strength of the Lord. We desire to know God is present with us in our need. Awareness of this need then yields new insight into the mystery and purposes of God for us.

We are familiar with the often-misapplied statement of Paul, "We know that God causes all things to work . . . for those who are the called according to His purpose. . . He predestined to be conformed to the image of His Son."[10] Note: Paul does not say God causes all things, rather He causes all things "to work." Father's objective is to

10 Excerpts from Romans 8:28-29

conform us as sons and daughters according to the Pattern Son. "All things" includes the "alien gifts". These must become objects of serious, active faith.

A Mystery

I am going to try my best to "pull back the curtains" on an amazing mystery from the unfathomable wisdom of Father. I say, "try", because I am still reaching to grasp the depth of it myself. The more I discover about the *strength of a position of weakness* (a counterintuitive oxymoron) the more I realize how many of the Kingdom mysteries are yet to be revealed.

I feel the weight of this message for two reasons. First, as the darkness becomes more aggressive against the people of God, it will be increasingly essential to live consistently in the power of the Spirit. Second, we may discover that in weakness we have been given a spiritual fortress that the enemy has no means of countering or penetrating.

Why would God choose to reveal Himself to the world through the weakness of a human baby born to an unmarried teenager? Why didn't the Messiah come to earth in the manner all Israel was expecting? Why would He not storm into Jerusalem as the conquering Son of David and establish it as the center of the nations?

To delve into the depths of these questions we need to settle two realities in our thinking. First, Jesus was born into a "spiritual Babylon" that was enslaving not only Israel but the entire world. The Kingdom of God brought redemption in contrast to the empire. Second, we must recognize the nature of God and how He chooses to govern His Kingdom redemptively within the context of "Babylonian" humanity.

Allow me to restate the cosmic battle lines again:

There are two spiritual "cities" under construction: Babylon and New Jerusalem. These two cities are the prototypes, representing the two governing systems of the inhabited earth:

- One has exerted its influence from Genesis to Revelation. It is named Babylon, "confusion." The sheer quantity of bible references to Babylon should not be minimized.
- The other city, identified as the New Jerusalem, has been in construction since before the foundations of the world.
- Conflict, warfare, and failure emerge from the long-standing conflict between these two entities.

My focus has been the Kingdom of God. As such, I have never delved as deeply into spiritual warfare as other ministries have been led to do. However, on the morning of July 24, 2021, I was enjoying coffee on my front porch with Judith when the palpable presence of the Lord surrounded me in a most extraordinary manner. As I was listening to the Spirit of the Lord, I suddenly became conscious of a dark, ominous presence moving beside me. The only way I can describe it is like a 16 mm film strip progressing vertically next to my right side. As it continued, it incrementally increased in strength and darkness until I was almost totally overwhelmed with the power of what I sensed. I am not unfamiliar with encountering the powers of darkness, but this was exceedingly stressful.

I came to understand that this darkness represented the "Babylonian Pantheon" of some 3,000 gods and goddesses. These forces of darkness have been present throughout human history. They oppose God and His purposes. But why would the Spirit of the Lord present this to me in the midst of His tangible presence and clarity of voice? I did not understand until later the magnitude of what He was intending. The Lord was desiring for us to comprehend more clearly a force that is too often unrecognized, yet pervasive and malevolent in its presence.

Babylon is a well-worn theme in our understanding as the corrupt spiritual world empire. Check Amazon and you will find that there are multitudes of books about America as the new Babylon, Babylon as the final world system predicted in Revelation, Babylon and the institutional church, and everything in between. In one way or another most teachings focus on Babylon as a central theme of popular eschatology. Therefore, you may be inclined to give a ho-hum yawn as we approach the subject. However, hang in there with me because Father is presenting a deepening, increasingly critical understanding of the sophisticated nature of this dark, insidious power.

Babylon is multi-faceted and pervasive. It is an atmosphere or culture; a value system; an energizing power; and a world empire. It is the antithesis of child-like. Its influence has the potential to control or corrupt every aspect of the human experience. The people of God are included; none are exempt. From the Charismatic preacher to the Pope in Rome, all are targets and potential victims.

I will unpack this as we go along, with one qualification. I will not try to fit Babylon into a prophetic pattern about who, when, where, and what develops before the consummation of the age. I do not wish to add to the present confusion. Principles defined and understood will be sufficient.

That being said, I do believe we are in an age-changing season of shaking and difficulty that will cleanse and transform the Church into a bride. She will be pleasing to Christ and awesome to the world. We will be challenged, could I say required, to leave a system of Christianity that emphasizes our personal interests and well-being. If we are willing to take up the yoke of Christ as it is being presented to us today, we will face the sober truth that it may be sacrifice that Christ expects.

When we approach Babylon, we are facing

something that is far more present, universal, and subtle than we have understood. We are being required to free ourselves from her intoxications. But first, allow me to lay some foundations.

For reasons that will become clear, I will use "Babylon" somewhat interchangeably with darkness, with this minor but important distinction. I will use Babylon as a form of illegal governmental force seeking control over humankind. I will use darkness, (Strongs Concordance #2217 used 5 times) as the deceptive power or force by which Babylon rules. Darkness encompasses anything and everything outside the knowledge of God. In the spiritual realm, darkness is not merely the absence of light as it is in the physical world. Spiritual darkness is a dynamic, malevolent entity, force, or influence that wages a constant assault on everything that is of God. Darkness can represent Satan and his minions (known in Scripture as the other gods); the functioning of the world system; or our untransformed human nature. This is how and why darkness is able use Father's own family against Him!

Using darkness, Babylon has three primary objectives: steal—kill—destroy: [11]

---

11 See John 10:10

1. **Steal the worship due to God alone.** The spirit of Babylon desired to be "like the Most High."[12] Lucifer envied the worship and honor being given to God and desired it for himself. He was willing to give up the kingdoms of the world if Jesus, as the incarnate Son of God, would fall down and worship him.

2. **Kill humanity.** Darkness has been a murderer from the beginning (John 8:44). As the objects of God's undeterred Agape, Babylon would like nothing more than to outmaneuver God by eliminating all humans from His creation. Millions have intentionally been killed.

3. **Destroy the image of God in the world.** Obviously, all the forces of darkness can never directly defeat God or turn aside His inexorable Agape. Therefore, the legions of darkness have focused much of their assault on God's *image and His name.* The forces throw every weapon at their disposal to destroy, dishonor, malign, and corrupt God's image before the eyes of the world and His own people.

Darkness incessantly attacks our identity as the image of God. As we look in our "spiritual mirrors,"

---

12 There is a belief that the 7 "I will's" of Isaiah were uttered by Lucifer. Other commentators and theologians believe that for contextual reasons this was actually uttered by the king of Babylon, or it is a representative declaration of the spirit of all the kings of Babylon. Whichever line is followed, it clearly represents the "spirit" of Babylon and the ultimate fate thereof.

we are often inclined to see our reflection as the first Adam. We see failures, short-comings, and sin. We often accept this as our "true" identity. Continual consciousness of sin and shortcomings is a work of darkness. *Our inheritance is to look into our "mirror" and see the image of the Son reflected back in us.* As the Spirit works through our faith, we become more conscious of His image in us.

Babylon – To Become Like God

Babylon is used throughout the Scripture to represent all that stands in opposition to God. The spirit of Babylon was present pre-creation in the heart of Lucifer. "You said in your heart, '. . . I will *make myself* like the Most High.'"[13] These words were attributed to the king of Babylon, identified as Satan by many Bible scholars. This same spirit enticed Adam and Eve, "You will be like the gods." The pursuit upward became the fall downward. Babylon and darkness entered the human race.

The conservative Biblical scholar, Edward Young, in his commentary on Isaiah wrote this concerning the passage:

> *Here is unbounded arrogance. How could the Babylonian spirit ever plan such a thing? The answer is that Babylon had sought to render void the work of God. God's plan was to bring salvation to the world through the coming of a Savior. Babylon had set herself*

---

13 Isaiah 14:14 [my italics]

in opposition to God; she would thwart His plans by means of self-exaltation against the true God.[14]

In Genesis 10:9, we encounter the Spirit of Babylon in the person of Nimrod, a "mighty hunter before the Lord."[15] He founded the city of Babel. The citizens desired to "make a name for themselves" by building a tower that would reach to heaven. This is the seed of self will, actively apart from God, which continues to be passed on and matured in coming generations. Babel symbolizes "idolatry, pride, self-reliance, the urge for material power, and the illusion of infinite achievement. It is a picture of misguided human aspiration."[16] Nebuchadnezzar, King of the Babylonian world empire, embodied and articulated this spirit when he boasted in his pride, "Is this not Babylon the great, which *I myself have built* as a royal residence by the *might of my power* and for *the glory of my majesty.*"[17]

The name Babylon means, "the gate of god," or "the gate of the gods."[18] The tower of Babel was the prototype of the Babylonian Ziggurats. A

14 Young, Edward J. *The Book of Isaiah, Vol. 1.* P. 442. ©1965, Eerdmans Publishing

15 *Nimrod* is rooted in the Hebrew word which means "we will revolt." – *Kiel and Delitzch Commentary on the Old Testament.*

16 "Babel, Tower of". *Dictionary of Biblical Imagery.* P. 66-67. ©1998 by Inter Varsity Press.

17 Daniel 4:30 [my italics]

18 Encyclopedia Britannica, 9th edition. Digital citation#182.

priest or priestess would ascend the Ziggurats to communicate with the local god or gods. These were counterfeits of the Tabernacle and later the Temple where Heaven and Earth meet as God's Presence.

In the Jewish Scriptures the spirit of Babylon ruled through the "other gods" and idols. In the New Testament, Paul identified Babylon as principalities and powers with whom the people of God are required to wrestle. Paul would have seen these as the Roman and Greek gods that commanded the corrupt aspects of Roman power, Greek philosophy, and Judaism. Apostolically, he called them world-dominators [Greek] of this darkness."[19]

In the book of Revelation, Babylon is prophetically revealed in full maturity. Here, "Babylon stands not for a specific power but more generally for world power in opposition to God— the empire where God's people live in exile."[20] Revelation pictures Babylon as a "whore" seducing the people of the earth away from the living God through illusions of fulfillment. Seduction is rarely blatant and forceful; it is subtle and enticing. "People usually do not enter rationally and deliberately into a situation of evil; rather, they are seduced into it."[21]

19 Ephesians 6:12
20 "Babylon." *Dictionary of Biblical Imagery.* P. 68-69. ©1998 by Inter Varsity Press.
21 Howard-Brooke, Wes & Anthony Gwyther. *Unveiling Empire.* ©1999 by Wes Howard-Brook & Anthony Gwyther. P1 166.

Seduction begins with deception. Eve, Paul says, was "deceived."[22] The Tree of the Knowledge of Good and Evil appeared to offer personal fulfillments. She could enjoy its beauty and flavor and improve her mind at the same time.

In the same verses, Paul warns against being led astray to "another Jesus" or a "different gospel" by which the Corinthians would receive a "different spirit." The gospel of "the other Jesus" looked good and sounded good, but in the end, they would be led astray from the Person of Christ. In a few pages we will look at seven motivations that make us vulnerable to seduction.

Biblically, Babylon represents the phenomenon of empire. The objective has always been domination and the increasing expansion of power. Empire is a relentless goal that can be pursued militarily, economically, ideologically, religiously, or politically. To really grasp how prominent this is in biblical human history, remember that Israel's story was played out in the shadow of Egyptian, Assyrian, Babylonian, Persian, Greek, and, ultimately, in the Roman Empire. For the most part, each of these empires dominated or enslaved the people of God, both Jewish and Christian.

In more recent history, during the sixteenth through the eighteenth centuries the nations of Europe battled to establish empires in the rest of the world. England, Spain, Portugal, France, and

---

22 See 2 Corinthians 11:3-4

the Dutch all vied, often violently, to establish empires in Africa, Asia, and the Americas. The colonial powers plundered, enslaved, and practiced genocidal murder throughout the world. This was rooted in greed and the lust for power. It was Babylonian in its motivations and goals.

The Greek word *basileia*, which we translate as kingdom, would have been understood to mean empire in the Greek and Roman world. Therefore, the early Christians were proclaiming the "Empire of God". Refusing to worship the Roman Emperor, Caesar, the Christians were seen as insurrectionists both religiously and politically.

Babylon is the dominating empire in our world system today. Its spirit infests and influences aspects of life on this earth, including, as we shall see, much of the visible church. For our purposes, we are more concerned about an atmosphere or climate than attempting to identify an entity.

I emphasized Babylon because it is critical that we understand that Jesus was born into a spiritual Babylonian empire. Israel was ruled through the darkness of Roman power, Greek philosophy, and religious legalism, arrogance, and manipulation. If Jesus had appeared as the expected messianic Son of David to renew the kingdom of David, *He would have inflamed the first century Jewish aspirations for power and recognition among the nations*.

The hearts of the nation would have been hardened in darkness rather than healed in the light of the accurate image of the glory of God. Therefore, the Messiah snuck in the back door. Jesus arrived as an infant; was laid in a feeding trough; and born to an unwed mother and a Galilean craftsman. He entered the world a common man among a common people. This may become clearer when we consider three unchangeable absolutes about God, the Father.

Our Foundation – God's Absolutes

For the sake of helping us work from a common foundation, we want to establish three biblical absolutes about God. These absolutes govern His posture toward humanity and His plans for the establishment of an earthly New Jerusalem.

First, His *creational sovereignty.* Because He created the cosmos and humankind, He is the owner of everything—nothing excluded. He governs freely, according to His pleasure. He is accountable to no one and nothing outside of Himself. He is subject to no ethical or moral judgements that we might apply to ourselves. He said it pretty clearly, "I AM WHO I AM."

Second, His *Agape.* Because God is love, all that He is and does is ultimately an expression of His Agape. *He does not have Agape, He is Agape!* Religious traditions often present God as having two sides: love and mercy on one side and anger and judgment on the other. All God is and does, even His judgments, are sourced in His love.

Third, His *relational mode of being.* Without someone to love, Agape becomes a moot point.

Love cannot exist in a vacuum. God has eternally existed as the Agape fellowship of Father, Son, and Holy Spirit. Mystics refer to this as "The Divine Dance." *God is determined to encounter us on a relational basis.* He is not content for us to know about Him or interact with Him on a transactional (religious) basis. He wants us to know Him and for us to be known by Him personally. He desires intimacy, reciprocation, and living communication. Before the foundation of the world, *He chose to create humanity in His image and include us in His circle of reciprocal Agape fellowship.* A hymn says it well:

> The universe of space and time did not arise by chance,
> But as the Three, in love and hope, made room within their dance.[23]

We can picture this graphically:

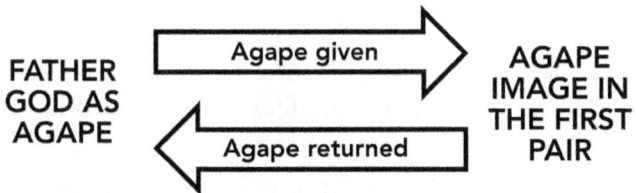

Figure 1
Agape Image at creation, returned to God.

---

23 "Come, Join the Dance of Trinity." Richard Leach

The relationship that God intended with the first pair was the return of His Agape image mirrored back to Himself. We could say that God created them using His own "DNA," which is His nature and character.[24] Adam and Eve were created human as God designed human beings to be. Being in the image of God, Adam and Eve were given personal sovereignty to subdue and fill the earth. They were able to live and work in absolute freedom from any influence other than God. Their sovereignty was to function within an Agape relationship with God and creation.

I would summarize the interworking of these absolutes of God's Person as follows: Out of His unchangeable *Agape,* the *Sovereign Creator chose* to redeem His family back into the *relationship* Himself. If we embrace these three absolutes as reality in our understanding and experience, then God's ways and workings in history and in us begin to come into focus.

The paradise of the Garden was "very good" until the serpent struck up a conversation with Eve about the possibility of being like God. The intricacies of this encounter are too familiar to warrant elaboration. Therefore, I will simply make one critical observation. Into this perfect environment of Agape love, Satan interposed a corrupted, counterfeit form of love, eros.

---

24 I believe the heart of God's DNA was expressed as He appeared to Moses in Exodus 34:6-7.

The following chart is from Anders Nygren's classic work, *Agape and Eros*.[25] .

Eros is acquisitive desire and longing.	Agape is sacrificial giving.
Eros is an upward movement.	Agape comes down.
Eros is man's way to God.	Agape is God's way to man.
Eros is man's effort: it assumes that man's salvation is his own work.	Agape is God's grace: salvation is the work of Divine love.
Eros is egocentric love, a form of self-assertion of the highest, noblest, sublimest kind.	Agape is unselfish love, it "seeks not its own"; it gives itself away.
Eros seeks to gain its life, a life divine, immortalized.	Agape lives the life of God, therefore, dares to "lose it."
Eros is the will to get and possess which depends on want and need.	Agape is freedom in giving, which depends on wealth and plenty.
Eros is primarily man's love; God is the object of Eros. Even when it is attributed to God, Eros is patterned on human love.	Agape is primarily God's love; God is Agape. Even when it is attributed to man, Agape is patterned on Divine love.
Eros is determined by the quality, the beauty and worth, of its object; it is not spontaneous, but "evoked", "motivated".	Agape is sovereign in relation to its object and is directed to both "the evil and the good"; it is spontaneous "overflowing", "unmotivated".
Eros recognizes value in its object—and loves it.	Agape loves—and crated value in its object.

25 Nygren, Anders's, *Agape and Eros*. Page 210, Westminster Press, 1932

As we will see, especially in a religious or humanistic setting, eros masquerades as Agape, producing all manner of laudable behavior but from a totally different motivation.

With the introduction of eros into humanity, the picture is transformed into something like this:

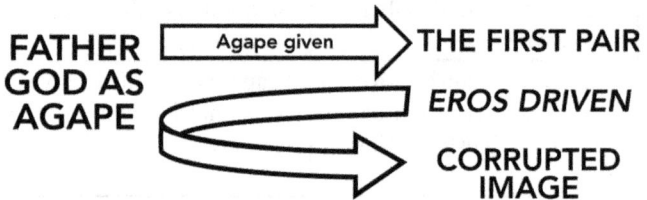

FATHER GOD AS AGAPE → Agape given → **THE FIRST PAIR** *EROS DRIVEN* **CORRUPTED IMAGE**

Figure 2

An eros-driven human takes the divine image and projects it back on himself. We are compelled to go our own way. Personal Sovereignty has been injured and corrupted. As we know from our understanding of human genetics, if the DNA of a person is corrupted, physical deformities and improper functioning of organs can and do occur. With the introduction of eros into our spiritual DNA, we were no longer able to function as God had intended. Regarding His image, we were "de-gened," hence the word, degeneration.[26] The results are vividly recorded in Romans 1:18-32.

26 "Having lost the physical, mental, or moral qualities considered normal and desirable; showing evidence of decline" Oxford Languages.

Scriptures attest to the creation of the human race in the image and after the likeness of God.[27] When Adam and Eve misused their personal sovereignty to "become like God," they severed the flow of life from their Creator. Personal sovereignty ceased being empowered by Agape. The first pair embraced their desire for personal aggrandizement. Eros empowered sovereignty produce the "right to myself as I desire".

The loss of God's Agape as an absolute demolished our human capacity to govern ourselves, or others. *Righteous, benevolent self-governing is only possible when abiding in the Creator's image and purpose*. Ironically, with the loss of Agape we are incapable of loving ourselves with the kind of love that enables us to make choices that produce life. We are either in control of ourselves through Agape, or we are being controlled by Babylonian darkness empowered by eros. The intrusion of eros produces fear, shame, and deception. A spiritual vacuum is created. The other gods enthusiastically fill the void with their own agenda.

Adam's failure has resulted in immeasurable human suffering. An agenda of ensuing darkness, deceiving, and manipulating all humanity has resulted. Blame and guilt are cleverly shifted toward God. He is accused and blasphemed as the one responsible for human suffering. Father is charged with a seeming lack of care and intervention. C.

27 Genesis 1:26; 2:7; 9:6.

Baxter Kruger explained:

> The human race is now lost in the most terrible darkness, the darkness of its own mind. It is locked into a cycle of anxiety and projection and misperception. The fallen mind not only projects its anxiety on the world and the people around it; the greatest disaster is that it projects its brokenness onto God's face.[28]

Please consider something that can bring great clarity to the age-long cosmic warfare in which we participate. The Babylon spirit declares, "I will make myself like the Most High." Notice the agenda is not to defeat, destroy, or de-throne God. It would be folly to wage war one on one with God, the omnipotent Creator! Allow this to sink deeply into our spiritual worldview. It is the cornerstone of Babylon: "Make myself like the Most High." This sounds strangely like Nebuchadnezzar's boast: "Is this not Babylon the great, which *I myself have built* as a royal residence by the *might of my power* and for *the glory of my majesty*."[29]

Satan lost his place of honor and glory in the presence of God. Cast down to the earth, he became as unlike God as a being could possibly become. Unable to raise himself up to be like God, he now

28 Kruger, C. Baxter. *Jesus and the Undoing of Adam*. Perichoresis Press. Kindle Edition.
29 Daniel 4:30 [my italics]

focuses his efforts on bringing God and Creation down to his level. Darkness distorts and dishonors God's image and name in an effort to alienate God and men.

The irony is that Satan wanted to become like God. Yet God, in the incarnation, desired to become like man.

Adam and Eve--Injury to Personal Sovereignty

By Adam and Eve's failure we lost our created, child-like innocence. The original pair forsook innocence for the knowledge of good and evil. As a result, we discovered ourselves to be naked. We now employ our "sovereignty" to cover our nakedness with our own glory. Our glory demands "my right to myself." This is both the source and the manifestation of our injured personal sovereignty. Living under Adam's curse, we are determined to go our own way and do our own thing. There are presently some eight billion human beings on the earth making erroneous decisions with their injured personal sovereignty. If you doubt that, think of the track record of all human history.

Following is an enlightening illustration from author Dan Scott:

My friend Leonard bought a truck.

"What a bargain," he thought, driving off the lot. He enjoyed how people admired his truck as he drove it around. The sound system was good. The leather seats were comfortable. The red paint was fresh and bright. The truck was great.

Except for one thing: the truck pulled to the left. No big deal. Leonard had the truck aligned. Then, he balanced the tires. Finally, a mechanic told him the truth: the truck's frame was bent.

The friendly salesman had failed to tell him the truck had been in a wreck. Although the body shop had worked wonders on the truck's appearance, it still had a bent frame.

Christianity teaches that every human being is born with a bent frame. Despite our best intentions, we pull to the side. Some people pull in one direction. Others pull in another direction. No one has a perfect frame. We are all born bent.[30]

The "bent frame" is our propensity to have our own way. I express myself as my own god. It is far more deeply entrenched than willpower, emotional commitment, mental agreement, or vows to do better can possibly root out. Darkness identifies, exploits, and manipulates the bent frame. Darkened personal sovereignty appeals to "*my right to myself*," with a

30 Scott, Dan. *Faith in the Age of AI*. Eleison Press. P. 199. © 2023 by Don Scott

skill that avoids detection—preventing our freedom.

In Adam, we are all born "bent." However, not everyone is bent in the same direction. Some are bent *left* with a propensity to be pulled into the secular world for identity, recognition, achievement, and control. Others are bent to the *right* choosing the religious or "spiritual" path to achieve the same ends. Whichever way we are inclined to pull, we soon discover our inability to cease running off the road.

Babylon harnesses the power of eros to illegally elevate human achievement. We pursue the "goodness of man" for our own happiness, health, and peace apart from God. Numerical increase and financial success in ministry, apart from Father's purpose, can lead to the Babylonian addiction of illegal recognition. Childlikeness is lost in the unrecognized propensity to move upward in pride where spiritual oxygen becomes scarce. Spiritual hypoxia clouds our thinking, and Godly decisions become difficult if not impossible.

Babylon is the empire where God's people live in exile. The violence and darkness of the human condition is appalling but is symptomatic of a deeper darkness. The heart of the modern Babylonian world view does not look to the "other gods" in the classical sense. Rather fallen man is set at the center—a god unto himself.

Oswald Chambers in *My Utmost for His Highest* states, "My claim to my right to myself, [is] the nature of self-realization which leads us to say, '*I am my own god*'"(October 5). When we confront "my right to myself" within ourselves, we are shocked to see how strongly we guard the "freedom" of our imagined sovereignty. We guard our "rights" at the supreme cost of losing our freedom to function in the Kingdom of God.

"I am the master of my fate; I am the captain of my soul"[31] is the declaration of our fancied right to personal sovereignty. This is a humanist world view. It dominates the operating foundation for the modern world, including much of Christianity. The Humanist Manifesto II states this quite succinctly, "As nontheists, we begin with humans not God, nature not deity. No deity will save us; we must save ourselves."[32] *Humanism uses what is good, to displace what is best.* This is darkness disguised as the "angel of light."[33]

Darkness emanates from a desire and an attempt to become like God. There is a truth here that we dare not fail to comprehend. The desired path of darkness is not downward, but upward. Eros centers on me and my sovereign authority. I make myself into whatever image I envision.

There is a form of religious humanism that takes the focus of our fellowship with the Lord to a false center. A false center, as we are using it, is doing the right thing for the wrong reasons. A team athlete

31 "Invictus,*"* William Ernest Henley
32 "Humanist Manifesto II," Published 1973
33 2 Corinthians 11:14

who performs solely for personal recognition may have personal success, but the team as a whole may suffer.

One false center for a believer is expecting God to fix all our difficulties in life. Our needs and problems become the hub of our interaction with Him. Blessings, financial prosperity, perfect health, freedom from failure and loss, perfect protection for family and friends are expected. All will be ours if we just have enough faith.

Another false center is endeavoring to "be a good Christian". We long to measure up to an image of what we believe the Lord (or church) wants or expects. We are hammered by the voice of "not enough." We need more prayer, more Bible, better discipline, better thought control, on and on and on. We are part of the "try harder club." Membership is free, but the dues are exorbitant, and the benefits are negligible. *Promises and principles have been substituted for the Person.*

Please don't misunderstand. I am not suggesting there is merit in living ignorant and undisciplined. The motivation for personal growth and development is part of the creative life force God has given us. However, motivation turns in on itself when bent by eros. Eros imprisons us within ourselves. Our rights to ourselves are closely protected by seven powerful Babylonian guards. Many of you will recognize them from my earlier works.

1. An ungoverned need to *look good*; spiritually, this is illegal recognition.[34]

2. An unrelenting pursuit of *feeling good;* avoiding, or masking discomfort.

3. A need to *be right*; defend my point of view.

4. An urgency *to control;* myself, situations, and others.

5. A *hidden personal agenda*; "What can I get out of this?"

6. An intent to *gain personal advantage*; procuring an upper hand.

7. A necessity to *remain undisturbed*; avoiding everything challenging my reality and comfort.

As innocuous as this list may seem at first glance, these are the openings for seduction into illusion and self-deception. Each contains the essence of eros. They are rooted in our bent frame. In truth, all of these are subtle manifestations of pride. Pride leads us away from childlikeness. These bends in our frame keep us focused on the service of our own desires and plans.

Tragically our bent frames limit the fullness of the power of Christ from expressing itself through us. My ability to enter the fulness of what the Father intends for me will be compromised. Leonard's

34 "Illegal recognition" is recognition which I solicit to meet my personal ego needs or to create an image.

truck with the bent frame will probably be fairly adequate for his daily needs. But, if he takes it on the highway at 70 mph or tries to negotiate the switchback curves in the mountains, he may find himself losing control and heading for the ditch. When life becomes demanding, the bent frame is revealed.

Illegal Recognition

Solicitation of illegal recognition may be the most tempting and damaging of all spiritual failures. The Scripture uses the term "hypocrite" to describe it. Hypocrite comes from a Greek word *hupokrites*, which "was an actor under an assumed character."[35] Actors become someone they are not in order to present an image of a particular role to their audience. In theatrics it is called, getting in character.

Jesus told the religious: "How can you believe, when you receive glory from one another and you do not seek the glory that is from the one and only God?"[36] And warned, "Beware of practicing . . . in order to be noticed." *Seeking glory from others is illegal recognition.*

In a religious community where conduct and character are admired and lauded, it is ever so easy to put on the religious, holy face of a "good Christian." How many of us have joined a group of fellow believers and automatically begun to "get

35 Strongs #5273
36 John 5:44

in character?" Jesus further warned His disciples, "Beware of the leaven of the Pharisees which is hypocrisy."[37] The unspoken pressure to "play the role," like yeast in a lump of dough, can spread through a community of believers like a bad case of flu. Justly or unjustly, the charge most often leveled against Christianity is hypocrisy.

Some years ago, I was led by the Lord to undertake a seven day fast. Fasting is not one of my favorite spiritual disciplines, but I did it from a sincere heart toward the Lord. Somewhere in the middle of the fast I happened to be in a group of several other pastors and leaders. We were discussing spiritual things and in the course of sharing my thoughts, I said, "Right now I'm doing a seven day fast." I subtly had the desire to appear very spiritual. Very gently I heard the voice of the Spirit whisper, "You just wasted seven days." I had a mental picture of the Lord taking something out of my basket, loss of reward. Ouch! I was seeking illegal, religious recognition.

The yearning for recognition can be an overwhelming drive. A nine-year-old boy once told me, "Mr. Mumford, you gotta know that having the police after you is better than having nobody know you." He would do things for the police to chase him, and then outsmart them. He was receiving recognition in life on his terms. I was in tears because I knew what he was saying—no family, no friends,

---

37 Luke 12:1

nobody. The need for identity and recognition helps populate gangs, cults, and extremist movements all over the world.

If we are motivated by one (or more, as is usually the case) of these seven Babylonian guards, eventually it or they will own us. We will become slaves. If we desire to look good within a group of peers, we will begin to align our words and actions to project the proper image. We will become slaves of that image—of another god.

The Assault

Because the omnipotent Creator cannot be defeated, the legions of darkness focus their assault God's *image* and *name*. Satan's strategy is being implemented on three battle fields.

First, as I have already said, Satan seeks to directly destroy humanity through violence and murder. He attacks every sphere of human existence: physical, intellectual, spiritual, and social. Graphic examples include: war, genocide, political oppression, and enforced poverty.

Second, Satan endeavors to deface the image of God within man. He seeks to enslave people to darkness and corruption. Worship of other gods, the occult, ungoverned lusts, addictions, and emotional wounding are among the schemes used to keep the glory of the image of God from coming to maturity in His created beings.

Third, Satan maligns and dishonors Father's

name before the world through the Babylonian influence on God's own people. This is perhaps the most subtle and insidious scheme. Beginning with Abraham, it has been God's design to reveal Himself and His redemptive Agape to the world through a people of His choosing. If darkness misrepresents and dishonors God through His own people, then His very person is discredited before a hurting and lost world. David's sinful, ungoverned lust with Bathsheba and the murder of Uriah "gave occasion to the enemies of the Lord to blaspheme."[38]

Darkened, untransformed personal sovereignty discovers how to use God's principles of growth and success apart from Father's person and approval—this is Babylonian success. We seek to use God and His gifts for personal gain and illegal recognition. We seek an "eros payoff". In direct contrast, the Lord desires to exercise His will and purpose through us when "the [Agape] of Christ controls us."[39] This distinction, while not obvious, is exceedingly determinative.

Oswald Chambers addresses this with his usual elegance:

> "Do not rejoice in this, that the spirits are subject to you" (Lk 10:20). Worldliness is not the trap that most endangers us as Christian workers; nor is it sin. The trap we __fall into is__ extravagantly desiring spiritual

38 2 Samuel 12:14.
39 Paul. 2 Corinthians 5:14.

success; that is, success measured by, and patterned after, the form set by this religious age in which we now live. Never seek after anything other than the approval of God.

In Luke 10:20, Jesus told the disciples not to rejoice in successful service, and yet this seems to be the one thing in which most of us do rejoice. We have a commercialized view—we count how many souls have been saved and sanctified, we thank God, and then we think everything is all right.[40]

Tragically, I could fill pages with stories of men and women who have brought dishonor and shame to the name of Christ and the church. Powerful ministries have been neutralized. And the Kingdom has suffered immeasurable losses. Often, it is sexual sin, financial manipulation, or an extravagant lifestyle brought to light and laid out for the world to see and scoff.

These tragedies do not appear out of nowhere. The Babylonian gods identify, water, and nurture "tares" in the soil of wounded personal sovereignties. The tares grow as the ministry grows. They prosper until they became a controlling power. For each of our sakes, and the sake of the Kingdom, we must understand Babylon and the only power capable of neutralizing its influence.

40 Chambers, Oswald. *My Utmost for His Highest,* April 24. © 1992.Oswald Chambers Publications Association.

This was graphically displayed in the life of Saul, the first king of Israel. Through the prophet Samuel, Saul was commanded to utterly destroy the nation of the Amalekites and all that they had. As it is recorded in 1 Samuel 15, Saul defeated the Amalekites through the power of God. But as we read the story, we see that Saul's wonderful victory was eclipsed by his eros-infected, bent frame. He disobeyed the Lord and dishonored Samuel.

We see these hallmarks of eros and subtle pride in Saul's conduct:

1. He spared King Agag, the cattle, and the sheep (vs. 9): corrupted personal sovereignty.
2. He set up a monument to himself on Mt. Carmel (vs. 12): pride, illegal recognition.
3. He erroneously believed that he had obeyed the Lord (vs.13, 20): deception.
4. He feared the people more than God (vs. 24): no fear of the Lord.
5. He wished to be honored before the people (vs. 30): false center.

Saul dishonored the command of the Lord, and he was rejected in regard to the Kingdom. Lest we think this is just the Old Testament version of God, Jesus would say to those who were following Him:

Not everyone who says to Me, "Lord, Lord," will enter the kingdom of heaven, but he who does the will of My Father who is in heaven will enter. Many will say to Me on that day, "Lord, Lord, did we not prophesy in Your name, and in Your name cast out demons, and in Your name perform many miracles?"

And then I will declare to them, "I never knew you; depart from me, you who practice lawlessness."[41]

Jesus' statement has nothing to do with Heaven or Hell. It speaks of His Kingdom. We enter by a relationship. We are bound by Agape and obedience. In these ministry tragedies, there was no real relationship. They operated apart from the restraint and motivation of Agape for Christ. They lacked a desire to bring honor to His name. We do not take this warning as seriously as we should. Remember, when Moses in his anger struck the rock with his staff, against the clear command of God the Father. Water still flowed at his command, irrespective of it being against Father's expressed will. However, it did cost Moses an earthly inheritance.

The principalities and powers subtly seduce the people of God. We become focused on demons, the antichrist, fentanyl, alcohol, Communists, or corrupt politicians. But that is only the surface strategy. *There is a more sophisticated agenda of bringing dishonor to the image and name of God through me and you*. Principalities and powers appeal to one or more of seven aspects of our bent frames. They lead

41 Matthew 7:21-23

good people into deadly behaviors without the full realization of where they will end.

I have come to understand why Jesus compared mammon to God Himself.[42] The seduction of wealth starts with Mammon promising us illegal recognition and power. The influence of this seduction is seen in the number of people who slavishly buy tickets to Powerball or Mega Millions each week. In their imaginations they picture the power, possessions, and pleasure that will be theirs' with the multiple millions. The reality is that they are about 300 times more likely to be struck by lightning. No wonder Jesus called it "the deceitfulness of riches."[43] A person may be morally, ethically, and religiously spotless but become ensnared in a sophisticated form of Babylonian deception.

In a religious setting we embrace all manner of spiritual disciplines to become more Christ-like. We reject the principles of the world and embrace biblical values. However, in spite of our best efforts, we may not be able to expunge the deepest roots of the Babylonian influence. It is quite possible that the ego that strove for recognition in the world, will simply move into a different realm. The need for illegal recognition can energize our spiritual ego.

Like Leonard's truck, which could not be repaired, the human race came from Adam with its "bent frame". Leonard needed to turn it in for

---

42 Matthew 6:24; Luke 16:13
43 Mark 4:19

demolition and buy a new one. Likewise, God consigned the Adamic race to "the scrap heap" and provided another Adam. He made all things new.

The second Adam brought to fruition the Father's purposes. Jesus offers total freedom from the influence of a bent frame. We lost the Father's DNA in the degeneration of the Fall, but He now offers for us to be "re-gened." By the new birth we are regenerated. Father replaces the eros corrupted DNA from Adam with the DNA of His Son. *It is for freedom that Christ set us free!*[44]

The Messiah Came in Weakness

As already mentioned, if the Messiah had appeared as the conquering Son of David, He would have fed the grandiose, self-referential aspirations of the Jewish nation. In the wisdom of God, Christ circumvented the great powers of this world by emptying Himself into the womb of a teenage girl. He entered the cosmos of human flesh as a common man.

Paul explained the mystery of the of God's wisdom in Christ when He wrote:

- For God's foolishness is wiser than human wisdom,
- And God's weakness is stronger than human strength,
- God chose what is weak in the world to shame the strong,

44   Galatians 5:1

- God chose what is low and despised in the world.
- Things that are not, to reduce to nothing things that are.[45]

If we pause and seriously examine what Paul is proclaiming, we hear the rumblings of a cosmic spiritual battle raging in the background. God's very presence invades the dominion of darkness and does that which darkness is incapable of doing:

- He *honors* the Father.
- He *loves* with Agape.
- He *serves*.
- He *gives* His life for the life of the cosmos.

He chose to function in weakness as the Son of Man. In stark contrast to the pomp and power of the earthly rulers, the eternal, all-creating Word chose to set aside His divine attributes. He emptied Himself into human flesh. He identified with our weakness. It was Christ's human weakness that revealed and defeated the skill, deception, and the corruption of Babylonian darkness.

In Jesus we see an authentic human. He functioned with the absence of a bent frame. He chose to walk in childlikeness with His father. Christ was free to hear the Father and respond in Agape. His humility defied all darkness and demonic activity.

As the Son of Man, Jesus intentionally identified

---

45 See 1 Cor.1:25, 27-28

with the outcasts, the poor, the widows, and the orphans. His humility and humanity attract the marginalized of the world. His unqualified, Agape-infused acceptance mirrors the Father's heart.

Phillip Yancy spoke to this in the story of his own personal quest for reality in *The Jesus I Never Knew*:

> Martin Luther goes further, speculating that throughout his life Jesus "conducted himself so humbly and associated with sinful men and women, and as a consequence was not held in great esteem," on account of which "the devil overlooked him and did not recognize him. For the devil is farsighted; he looks only for what is big and high and attaches himself to that; he does not look at that which is low down and beneath himself."[46]

We may or may not be able to fully agree with Luther. But his understanding of the nature of Christ's incarnation helps clarify one of the most simple yet profound insights into the opposing dynamics of the cosmic epic: rebellion came into existence when Satan coveted to make himself like God. Redemption came into existence when God wanted to make Himself like a man. Witness the "upside down" Kingdom:

46 Yancey, Philip. *The Jesus I Never Knew* (p. 71). Zondervan. Kindle Edition.

- Exalt yourself (Babylonian) and you will be brought down.
- Humble yourself (Kingdom) and you will be exalted.

The Father chose to exercise His creational sovereignty in quiet, humble Agape. Why? His highest value is a relationship with His creation. If He had merely wanted control and obedience, a myriad of heavenly warriors and a little fire and brimstone would have been more than sufficient. *He wants our person more than our performance.*

He gives us choices rather than demands. He offers us His own life and fellowship in covenantal faithfulness. He responds to our needs and failures as a Father, not as an autocratic perfectionist. He uses any means necessary to dissolve our darkened, delusional "realities" to allow us the freedom to choose the path of transformation. Father's goal is always relational restoration. He seeks personal intimacy rather than perfect behavior.

Weakness Matters

Returning to our theme of childlikeness, we might ask ourselves if Jesus, as our example, ever demonstrated child-like weakness? He always seemed pretty together and mature. We know Jesus was crucified because of weakness.[47] However, the weakness at the hands of His tormentors

---

47 2 Corinthians 13:4

was preceded by a more profound and intimate demonstration of His true humility.

I would like to take some literary license to open what I believe to be the very nature of Jesus' interaction with His Father in the garden of Gethsemane. Jesus said His soul was grieved in agony to the point of death. The gospels record that He prayed "fervently". His sweat was like drops of blood. He knew exactly what He was facing. He had witnessed the horror of crucifixion many times. We should never put Jesus in His agony on some kind of heroic pedestal. He was thoroughly human. His humanity recoiled at the spiritual, emotional, and physical agony He was about to endure.

In the garden Jesus addressed His Father as "Abba." This is Aramaic for something close to Papa. It is a term an adult child would use in expressing the personal intimacy of a relationship. This is the only time recorded in scripture that Jesus addressed His Father in this manner.

In John 5:20, Jesus says, "The Father loves the Son." This text uses the Greek, *phileo,* which expresses love for a friend. Jesus appealed not only to His Papa, but also His friend as a mature Son. It is the deepest personal connection possible. "Papa, you can do anything! If possible, I wish you would take this cup away from Me. However, your wishes are more important than my wishes. "

The second request, for some reason, I picture Jesus embracing His Father with His face buried in His Father's shoulder. "My Father. I know if I simply asked, You would dispatch twelve legions of angles to come to my rescue. However, if that is not your wish, then I will drink this cup."[48]

Please note I have not used the word "will" in the conversation as most translations do. Wish or desire more accurately expresses the nuance of the Greek word. The Father did not demand that Jesus go to the cross. Jesus had a choice, which evidently, the Father would have honored. The Son of Man chose the place of weakness, for which the Father "highly exalted Him."[49]

Jesus, as the last Adam, accomplished something Satan and his minions were incapable of doing. He presented the Father with the honor He was due. Christ honored His Father and His Father honored Him. He raised Jesus from the dead. *The Son's weakness and obedience released the power of God without limits.* This is the image the Father is working to perfect in us.

Christ's obedience broke the curse of the first Adam. A new creation and a new race of mankind was born. A new supreme authority was now present on the earth. An authority to subdue the world system in obedience to God's inevitable Kingdom's triumph.

I was given a life-lesson in the "strength" of weakness while I was still in seminary. I was

48 Mumford paraphrase, Luke 22:42-44
49 See Philippians 2:9-11

waiting for a pastor friend at his church when a man walked in off the street and said, "I need to talk to somebody."

As soon as he sat down, I was aware of a dark, satanic presence filling the room. I asked, "Who are you? What's your name?"

He stared at me and said, "No, you don't need to know my name."

As he said this, I saw his face changing into horrible features. Then his tongue started to shoot in and out like a serpent, and he said, "Can you help me?"

Immediately the Lord said to me, "Don't touch him! Dismiss him right now and ask him to leave."

So, I said, "Sir, I don't know anything about this. I can't help you."

He said, "Okay." His face became normal again, and he walked out.

After he left, I was physically exhausted. I began to realize that God's faithfulness had saved me from getting a good thrashing.

Later, I became aware that *the defense mechanism the Lord had directed me to take had been humility and weakness*. I had been challenged to a fight that I would have lost. I was being tempted to be "God's man of power and authority" beyond what I was mature enough to handle. My spiritual ego was all set to kick in. Babylonian triumphalism does not back down from a fight.

Christ posture of genuine humility and weakness

had "disarmed the powers and authorities, [making] a public spectacle of them, triumphing over them by [the weakness of] the cross."[50] Through the new birth, He offers all mankind the opportunity to join the new race, set free from the curse of sin and death. We are free to accept His yoke in serving humanity in the power of weakness.

Some of you may be thinking, "Bob's getting a little obsessive about this weakness kick. Maybe it's just a projection of his advancing age?" Believe me, I am well aware that this theme cuts across the grain of popular teaching. It is much more enticing to offer a sure-fire formula on how to develop a power-filled ministry, prayer life, or church growth project. I surely don't want to detract from the genuine desire to accomplish Christ's mission through the present power of God. My concern is that I have watched the Babylonian influence creep into the anointed men and women of God.

He/she begins to build "my" ministry, church, or home group. Subtly he basks in the honor and recognition of success. Babylon has planted a seed. Success in ministry can be intoxicating. It can lead to addictive behavior. We yearn for more, bigger, and better. How do I know? Let's just say I have had a "taste the wine of success" at times in my years of ministry and the Lord has had to "sober me up" through weakness.

---

50 Colossians 2:15, NIV. [Brackets mine]

Examples of Why Weakness Matters

The weakness of Christ was not unique in the redemptive progress of God. The uniqueness of Jesus was that *He chose the path of weakness.* Let's look back at how this theme of weakness has appeared as an integral part of God's bringing men or women to the fulness of His purpose. I will take one example from the Old Testament and one from the New Testament.

Abraham

Abraham was in some ways God's first "invasion" of the empire of the other gods. Abraham was given a fairly heady promise by God. He would become a great nation, be greatly blessed, have a great name, and bless all the nations!

Abram (his name at this point) was about 75 years old at the time. He related the promise of a Son to Sarai, which presented a problem because Sarai was barren. They continued to work at having a child for the next fifteen or sixteen years. Finally, Sarai had an idea. She suggested that Abram fulfill the promise with Hagar. Abram agreed, and Hagar gave him Ishmael. By this time Abram was about 86 years old.

Thirteen years later God appeared to Abram, who was now 99 years old. He made a covenant of circumcision. Abram's name was changed to Abraham, and Sarai become Sarah. It was time; Sarah would give Abraham a son. It is recorded that they both laughed at the promise. "You've got to be kidding! We've been at his for thirteen years without success. Now when we are not really that lively anymore, You really expect us to do this!"

Not a very reverent response to the promise of a miracle. However, they were not laughing at God. They were laughing at their own weakness. As Paul records in Romans, Abraham "contemplated his own body, now as good as dead since he was about a hundred years old, and the deadness of Sarah's womb."[51] In faith they gave their weakness to God. Isaac was born according to promise, and history was changed forever.

This dynamic was also apparent in the lives of two other pivotal figures in Israel's history—Moses and David.

Paul

Saul of Tarsus was a leading figure in first century Israel. His political stature, piety, lineage, education, and zeal had elevated him as a predominant figure in the effort to suppress the growing cult of Christianity. He thought Jesus of Nazareth was a false Messiah.

Christ confronted Saul as he was heading to Damascus, and Saul's neat, undisturbed world was shattered beyond recognition. He found himself physically and spiritually blind in ultimate spiritual and theological weakness.

---

51 Romans 4:19

Paul testified that during his personal chaos, God "was pleased to reveal His Son in me." He received a revelation of the mystery hidden throughout the ages of redemptive history. He was foremost among those who would "upset the world" as a steward of the New Creation. He expounded and declared the mystery of Christ.

However, in spite of the power of God flowing through him, he continued to operate in weakness. He wrote to the Corinthians, "I was with you in weakness and in fear and in much trembling."[52]Rather than despise his weakness, Paul told the Corinthians, "If I have to boast, I will boast of what pertains to my weakness."[53] I have heard a lot of preachers over the years reference weaknesses, but I have yet to hear any boast about it. Me included.

What did Paul understand about his weakness that allowed him to embrace it? In the next chapter, Paul unpacks the purpose and power of weakness:

> Because of the surpassing greatness of the revelations, for this reason, to keep me from exalting myself, there was given me a thorn in the flesh, a messenger of Satan to torment me—to keep me from exalting myself! Concerning this I implored the Lord three times that it might leave me. And He has said to me, "My grace is sufficient for you, for power is perfected [Lit. "ends"]

52 1 Corinthians 2:3
53 2 Corinthians 11:30

in weakness." Most gladly, therefore, I will rather boast about my weaknesses, so that the power of Christ may dwell [lit. "tabernacle"] in me. Therefore I am well content with weaknesses, with insults, with distresses, with persecutions, with difficulties, for Christ's sake; for when I am weak, then I am strong.[54]

There are five points here which are essential to our theme:

First, the context is the "greatness of the revelations" Paul received as referenced earlier.

Second, Paul was given a thorn in his flesh, a messenger from Satan that tormented him. Paul's use of the thorn image is probably drawn from the warning to Israel that their enemies would be "thorns in their sides"[55] if they failed to completely remove the inhabitants of the land. There are endless speculations as to what the thorn might have been, but the only thing we need to know is that it was tormenting enough that Paul petitioned the Lord three times to have it removed.

Third, Paul mentions twice that the "alien gift" was intended to keep him from "exalting himself." This implies that God was protecting Paul from the efforts of darkness to appeal to his bent frame. Paul was vulnerable to illegal recognition. He had lived <u>most of his life</u> subject to the Babylonian influence

54 2 Corinthians 12:7-10
55 Numbers 33:55

of self-made righteousness, academic excellence, Greek wisdom, and Roman citizenship. Paul had employed these in "advancing in Judaism far beyond many of my contemporaries."[56] He was still vulnerable to running off the road.

Fourth, in Paul's weakness his own power came to an end. The NASB English text reads, "power is perfected [ends] in weakness." Every other English translation I checked inserts the pronoun "My" before "power" indicating that it is God's power that is perfected. The NASB, however, correctly does not.

You will notice that I have inserted a bracketed "ends" after "perfected" in the above quote. It is *Paul's power that <u>ends</u> in weakness; rather than God's power being <u>perfected</u> in Paul's weakness.* Is this important? Yes! First, God's power is perfect. It has no need of being more perfect. Second, the issue at stake is that if Paul were to begin using the power of God to gain illegal recognition it could endanger the purity of the gospel and himself. The technicalities of reading this as I do would take us away from our intended line of thought. However, if you are inclined to dig deeper, I have included an appendix from another author who explains it in excellent exegetical detail.

Fifth, Paul makes the astounding statement that he would gladly boast in his weakness. He was content with all manner of weakness and difficulty

---

56 Galatians 1:14

for Christ's sake. Why? He desired Christ's power to "tabernacle" in him. Paul was not envisioning a special outpouring of the Spirit when he was ministering. *He longed for the power of Christ to take up residence in him continuously.*

A different form of "tabernacling" is used in John 1:14. John declared that the Word became flesh and "dwelt" with us. The incarnate Christ did not come and go according to the need of the moment—He took up residence with us. "God has moved into the neighborhood."[57] Permanent residence on earth with His human family has been the Father's desire from the beginning.

Paul understood his present human weakness as something appearing negative. But when he accepted it with active faith, it yielded positive fruit. It produced insight and vision inaccessible in any other way. He embraced persecutions, all manner of physical abuse, and repeated prison encounters, without which we would not be in possession of his prison epistles.

The unrecognized "alien gift" functions something like this: God permits, but does not cause, suffering. Paul's unexpected yet deeply rewarding result was a dramatic increase of spiritual vision with the eyes of his heart (Eph. 1:18). Some will refuse and rebel at such a proposal. Others will see Paul, by faith, expressing pent-up gratitude for such insight.

---

57 Revelation 21:3. The Message

Bob Mumford

My own "alien gift" of human weakness was encountered in 1984. Up until then, I was recognized as a leading figure in the Charismatic outpouring, both in the United States and other parts of the world. I felt as though I was on the leading edge of all God was doing in His Kingdom! However, beginning in the late 1970's, my ministry began to stagnate. Many of my relationships in the larger Body of Christ were lost. This culminated in a geographic relocation from Ft. Lauderdale, which further traumatized both Judith and me.

My strong will, human determination, and crusade-like disposition unexpectedly crashed and burned. I was left emotionally and spiritually devastated. This season included a discipline of necessary corrections. My Babylons were being systematically dismantled. There were months, not weeks, of tears and mourning. I thought I really would die, both physically and spiritually.

In the midst, Father's "alien gift" appeared in the form of a direct, unqualified request: Will you follow Biblical Agape wherever it leads you? Will you embrace, with joy, the personal cost that such obedience will require?

First, I gave a mere verbal yes. Though I was most apprehensive about what might follow, I knew better than to say no to an offer from the Father. This response was soon followed by a deep, internal yes. Then a plethora of affirmations poured from my weakened person: my personal sovereignty said, "Yes!" And my behavior began to say, "Yes!"

Now, forty years later, I am testifying to the value of His "alien gift". *Father's weakness is stronger than any known human strength.* My Kingdom eyes were opened in ways that would not have been possible apart from His personal, fatherly, intervention. "Thank you, Father, for Your alien gift!"

Let Me Be Clear . . .

Before moving to a personal application of this in our own lives, I need to be sure that something is clear. When I speak of embracing our weakness and presenting it to the Father, I am not implying that we become personal wimps. We don't helplessly lie on our backs and allow darkness, people, and circumstance to run rough-shod over us. The Scripture continuously encourages and commands strength, endurance, courage, standing firm, not turning back, pressing on, and the exercising of our legitimate authority in Christ. There is an inner strength that does not come from our human strength. This strength comes from our being "in Christ". As Paul would write to the Ephesians, "Be strong in the Lord and in the strength of His might."[58]

One of life's most critical lessons is human weakness properly understood and embraced. *Our weakness becomes a conduit that releases the <u>power of Christ</u> in us without damage to ourselves.*

58 Ephesians 6:10

It is intended to lead us into childlikeness before God. Weakness protects us from the enticements of Babylonian self-empowerment.

The power of the Spirit flowing through us can be intoxicating. The illegal use of it, tragically, has led many to open ruin. When this happens, dishonor and embarrassment are reflected on God's person, His name, and the church. This is the design of the forces of darkness. I have watched wonderful ministries fail because the "eros guards" were never conquered. The ever increasing need to be satisfied eventually gave the guards control of the steering wheel—and all ended up in the ditch.

In the lives of most of us, the consequences are not so dramatic. Giftings and callings continue to function and bear fruit. But with the presence of well-hidden and fiercely defended eros strongholds, fruit may be limited to a thirty-fold or sixty-fold increase. Without our knowing, the subtle influence of darkness may form an illusion in our minds. We believe we are living in truth and integrity while defending illusions with selective Bible verses. In my years of ministry, I have found that this form of self-deception is almost impenetrable.

The secret to Jesus' freedom from the Babylonian influence is clearly stated in Philippians 2:6-8. This was His "kenosis" [Greek, self-emptying], placing Himself in a sphere of humility, obedience, and weakness. The prevailing powers of darkness could not penetrate this realm. Full, unqualified self-emptying embraces our weakness. We return to innocence and childlikeness.

Our objective is to eliminate and guard against the influence of Babylon and the world system. *Human weakness, properly understood and embraced*, constitutes a sphere in which the forms of negative influence appear to be powerless. By departing from humility and innocence, we become increasingly susceptible to the influence of darkness. Illegal recognition, building personal kingdoms, using the ministry as a means of excessive affluence, and a triumphalist mind set cannot overcome genuine biblical weakness.

Jesus washed the disciples' feet saying, "What I am doing you do not realize." Christ had entered a sphere of humility that the Babylonian powers are incapable of imitating or influencing. Therefore, He commanded His disciples: Wash each other's feet and love each other as I have loved you.

The world recognizes we are Father's kids because we are free. Humility, obedience, and weakness set us apart from the Babylonian powers and institutions. Darkness is powerless to penetrate these. Jesus desires that the world be discipled by us washing feet, not by imperialistic evangelism.

Discerning Weakness

There are different kinds of weakness we encounter in our lives that allow Christ to reveal His glory in and through us. On the cross, Christ's weakness before His Father and in the eyes of the world, ushered in the Kingdom through the power revealed and released in the resurrection.

Weakness of Peter

Peter's denial of Jesus is a weakness we would wish to avoid. And we assume, like Peter, we never would. But this weakness seems inevitable. It is weakness we will feel when we fail Christ. Our attempts at courage and faith, though sincere, are inadequate. This is not for lack of love or authenticity. We are just trying to get spiritual legs to walk. Peter's spirit was willing, but his flesh was still weak. Because Christ is faithful to correct and rebuke, we can take comfort that even in our weakness He will not give up on us. Peter returned to receive forgiveness. This is the Kingdom response. The center of Peter's focus was His relationship with Jesus.

Judas' response to his failure in betrayal was different. His heart was imprisoned by Babylonian greed. Due to this bend in his frame, instead of responding in humility, he responded in a despairing pride. He avoided responsibility for his weakness and ended his own life.

Jesus demonstrated with Peter His willingness to embrace our weaknesses and mature them into strengths. However, Jesus will not allow us to use weakness as an excuse to remain weak, ignorant, and immature.

Weakness of Imprisonment

One aspect of Paul's weakness was his imprisonment. This weakness seemed counter-productive to what he was called to do for the Kingdom. As an apostle, he was to declare the gospel of the Kingdom to the Gentiles and plant churches.

There are "imprisonment seasons" in which we may appear to be losing spiritually or falling behind. This kind of weakness directly opposes the world's definition of "success." However, Paul's imprisonment served to advance the Kingdom by the epistles he wrote. He received deep revelation because of his weaknesses.

In our own religious pride, we may struggle against such weaknesses. We might consider ourselves to be losing. But that is not the story the cross tells. In childlikeness, we can learn to surrender our weakness. We can allow it to serve us rather than attempting to pray our way out of it. What if Jesus had prayed His way out of Gethsemane rather than praying through it to glory?

How Do I Offer Father My Weakness?

The Apostle Peter writes, "God is opposed to the proud, but gives grace to the humble. Therefore, humble yourselves under the mighty hand of God that He may exalt you at the proper time."[59] Humility is a posture we are continually asked to

59 1 Peter 5:5-6

embrace for ourselves. In Scripture, it is expressed in different ways: obedience, yielding, taking the yoke, serving, and submitting. We think of faith, hope, and love as paramount spiritual postures, but I would suggest that humility is the precursor to each of these. *Childlikeness, innocence, and identity are all discovered and maintained in humility*. Please note Peter tells us there is a time element involved. The time of "exaltation" comes when the Father knows we are able to handle it without running off the road.

I am beginning to believe that in many instances the alien gift of weakness may be the Father's invitation to join the loving circle of humility and preference within the Trinity. Therefore, embracing and surrendering my human weakness to God as my Abba Father is far more urgent. *This involves an outright recognition and intentional response of yielding my right to myself to God.* However, as the saying goes, "It's easier said than done!" I cannot adjust my bent frame any more than Leonard could fix his truck's bent frame with his tool kit from Advance Auto Parts!

The bend in the frame of Leonard's truck was well hidden. The Babylonian culture working in us is often so familiar that we do not recognize it for what it is. The Babylonian guards have literally become part of our personality. A way to identify them is our reaction when one of them is not recognized and "properly served." Hurt, resentment, anger, indignation, withdrawal, anxiety, blame, and fault-finding are all indicators that the expected eros gratification was denied. These are the symptoms of the influence of Babylon.

We try all kinds of religious things to "keep the car on the straight and narrow." Confess more scripture, pray more in the Spirit, go to another conference, fast—the list of ways to improve ourselves is endless. These may be helpful, but for the most part they will not keep the car from continuing to pull. There is a better way!

Through the Spirit of Christ, you have been *invited to receive and embrace the Government of God*. Presented by and in Jesus Christ, God's government establishes your identity and reality. Christ's spirit within you begins His intercessory cry, "Abba! Father!"[60] It is the longing of a child reaching for Papa.

Embracing our human weakness enables us to truly yield to the gracious gift of God's fatherhood as government. *Human weakness is NOT failure!* Our human weakness is not only a place of safety, but also a spiritual weapon. But let's be clear. It is our weapon against the Babylonian darkness that seeks to enslave us. When you recognize weakness, do not run from it, deny it, or try to make it go away with more effort. Go to your Father!

---

60   Romans 8:15; Galatians 4:6

Conclusion

Becoming childlike is a powerful spiritual dynamic. We are exiles in a Babylonian empire founded on human wisdom and soul-strength. This empire seeks to displace God as the Lord of creation and bring all glory and honor to itself. Humanity and creation have struggled under the oppression of its present darkness.

Creation waits and groans for the glory of our freedom from Babylon. The glory of the Father shines out through our "washing of feet" as we serve in humility as sons and daughters. The power of the tabernacled Christ in His people brings glory to the Father's image and name "that God may be all in all."[61]

If this presentation of the proper place of weakness has awakened a new measure of reality in you, would you take some serious time to meditate on the five points below? As you are able, begin an active quest to make them a living possession in your own experience.

1. With active faith, be willing to embrace the reality that we are often unable to see the strength of our own self-delusions.

2. Repeatedly be willing to acknowledge the bends in our frames—both secular and religious.

---

61 1 Corinthians 15:28

3. Without reasoning or justification, cease all religious efforts to straighten our bent frames. Paul warned the Colossians that though such efforts may have "the appearance of wisdom," they will prove to be futile. They will be revealed as inadequate, "defrauding [us] of [our] prize."[62]

4. Honestly and courageously confront the "all things" that reveal our weaknesses. Refuse to run, hide, or shift blame.

5. As a child, offer weakness to the Father as Christ did. Jesus gave Himself in weakness washing the feet of the twelve, Judas included. He said: "You do not realize now what I am doing, but later you will understand."

Finally, would you join me in offering our weakness together to the Father:

God, my Father, I present myself to you as your child. I thank you that in your loving providence you are working through "all things" to conform me to the image of your Son. Thank you that Christ's power resides in me. Allow me to experience the lessons

62 See Colossians 2:16-23

of weakness that Jesus promised we would learn later.

Would you receive my apology for believing that my own doctrinal limitations would alter your sovereign response to those who are hurting? I release you to be God to others as you have been God to me.

For that purpose, I present my deepest self to you. Reveal and release me from all forms of darkness including those I entertain for self-preservation. I offer my weakness that I might join the "foot-washing" cadre that brings honor and glory to your name.

LIFECHANGERS®

P.O. Box 3709 ❖ Cookeville, TN 38502
931.520.3730 ❖ lc@lifechangers.org

APPENDIX

Excerpt from *Powers, Weakness, and the Tabernacling of God*, by Marva J. Dawn.

(The Greek text of 2 Cor. 12:9 contains no pronoun in connection with the *dunamis*, "the power.") Interpreting the power as Paul's rather than God's leads to significantly different theological conclusions that are very important here for our discussion of being Church in a world characterized by the workings of various principalities and powers.

Utilizing several related word studies, my M.Div. thesis explored the distinction between the two verbs *teleo* and *teleioo*—the former meaning primarily "to end, finish," and the latter involving a wide range of connotations, including "to perfect, to make genuine, to complete, to succeed fully, to initiate, to make happen, to become." The latter is used nine times in the letter to the Hebrews, which portrays Christ as the perfect fulfillment of the priesthood and the tabernacle. *Telex*, on the other hand, is used frequently in the book of Revelation, which includes many instances of terminating something, or carrying something out to the full. Paul uses the verb *teleioo* only once, and he uses it to emphasize that he has not reached the state of perfection implied by the verb. Rather, he insists, he continues to run his course and to discipline himself in order to press on toward the mark of the upward calling of Jesus Christ (Phil. 3:12-13).

The verb *teleo* seems to be more limited in its connotations. Out of twenty-eight instances in the New Testament, twenty-five times it is translated with verbs signifying some sort of finishing or ending or accomplishing. Of the remaining three, two appearances of the verb are related to taxes (Matt. 17:24 and Rom. 13:6) and reflect a common idiom, "to complete the taxes," which corresponds to our expression "pay taxes." The only other instance is the one in 2 Corinthians 12:9, which has always been rendered "to make perfect." It is my contention that this instance should not be excepted. Rather, the verb *teleo* here should be given the usual rendering, "to finish." Such a rephrasing would allow us to develop more clearly an understanding of the concept of God's power at work in human weakness.

Here is a listing of all the usages of *telex* in the New Testament:

Matthew 7:28: Now when Jesus had finished saying these things

Matthew 10:23: "you will not have gone through [finished going to] all the towns ..."

Matthew 11:1: Now when Jesus had finished instructing his twelve disciples

2 Corinthians 12:9: My grace is sufficient for you, for power is made perfect in weakness

[NOTE: for the sake of space, I have not listed twenty-two citations Dr. Dawn included. These three I have left as an example as well as her last one which is necessary for properly understanding her argument. – Bob Mumford]

Does not that last translation seem erroneous, in light of all the preceding usages? Certainly, this list suggests that, though the verb *teleo* is obviously rich in nuances, it is indeed quite consistent in always being employed to indicate some sort of finishing, completing, ending, or accomplishing - rather than the perfecting or maturing of the verb *teleioo*. Why should 2 Corinthians 12:9, then, be translated as if the verb there were *teleioo*? It seems that the practice is so entrenched that scholars have a difficult time imagining an alternative.

For the rest of this chapter, we will assume that 2 Corinthians 12:9 should be translated with the sense of "ending." What are the advantages to be gained from rendering the verb *teleo* in this way?

It seems to me that to do so makes more sense of the relationship of human weakness to God's power. See how you respond to this translation of Paul's description in 2 Corinthians 11:30 and 12:7-10:

If it is necessary to continue boasting, I will boast of those things which show my weaknesses.... Therefore, to keep me from being too elated, a thorn in the flesh was

*given to me, a messenger of Satan to knock
me about, to keep me from being too elated.
Three times I appealed pealed to the Lord
concerning this, that it might depart from
me, but he said to me, "My grace is sufficient
for you, for [your] power is brought to its
end in weakness." All the more gladly, then,
will I boast in my weaknesses that the power
of Christ [not mine!] may tabernacle upon
me. Therefore, I take delight in weaknesses,
in insults, in necessities, in persecutions and
calamities for the sake of Christ, for when I
am weak, then I am strong.*

The goal is for our power to come to its end.
Marva J. Dawn, M.Div.; Ph.D. *Powers, Weakness,
and the Tabernacling of God.* © 2001 by Eerdmans
Publishing. Locations 414-449, Kindle Edition.

NOTE: *Some of the discrepancies which Dr. Dawn
describes can be attributed to the different Greek
texts used for the King James Bible and the more
modern translations such as the NASB and NIV.
More recent translations are based on Greek texts
older (and assumed to be closer to the original
Greek texts) than the ones used by the 1611 King
James translation. However, in some instances
(such as this one) the modern translations have
followed the preferences of the King James for the
sake of traditional understanding. – Bob Mumford*